MONK *on a* HIL

PRAISE FOR *MONK ON A HILL*

'These are delicate, sensual poems of inwardness and solitude, but also of place and people. There are startlingly tender accounts of love and grief and a brooding lyricism brought to the description of towns and Himalayan history. A wonderful first collection.'—Anjum Hasan

'Guru Ladakhi is a visionary who has a world to reveal to us. In an age fragmented between the abstract universalism of the computer screen and the parochial, Ladakhi is a fortunate traveller, equally at home in the Musee d'Orsay and in the Buddha's birthplace. Ladakhi is a master of hard-earned lyricism, "spitting out the residue of lilies", always alert to contradiction, "to the reality check/of the refugee camp". His collection is put together musically: motifs recur, modulate, deepen. Ladakhi plays for high stakes: this is poetry that aims to recover a human reality even as globalization erases our landmarks, even if "we live fugitive lives forever".' —Dennis Nurkse

'*Monk on a Hill* comes at you like a ship on the horizon with pennants flying in the wind. These poems bear the insignia of diverse kingdoms, continents and journeys unfurling in unexpected ways the truth about time, memory; of fathers and sons, of mothers and heirlooms, "what a maze the years have been".

'There is music here, "a dozen songs in 12-bar blues", and devotion, "I who have grown like a rock here/witnessed every grass and cloud that passed", where images combine with text to give meaning to the vision of the poet that is, in short, "very cool" and, at the same time, thought-provoking, with an essence of spirituality. These are words from the heart. Beautiful. Evocative. Ponder this in 'The Old Monk of Sonada': "just before we take leave he says, 'be happy!'/ suddenly, like a thunder shower, I know".'—Mamang Dai

'People, places, postscript name the three sections into which Guru T. Ladakhi's poems in *Monk on a Hill* are emotively divided. As a visual imagist, Ladakhi is adept at evoking scenes and feelings with short, descriptive lines and sensual similes. At times such compressed beauty suggests transience and decay—men and women, too, fade away and die:

> "Daisy's world shuts around her,
> she floats from room to room
> looking for a mysterious key
> that refuses to open."

'In these poems one senses that the poet's blood is sum and substance with nature's flow; nature remains always as a subtle mirror. This small volume of poems contains a world of confidences that have been beautifully articulated in a fine poetic sequence.'—Jayanta Mahapatra

MONK *on a* HILL

~ poems ~

Guru T. Ladakhi

SPEAKING TIGER

To my mother who was devoted
and my father who was wise

SPEAKING TIGER BOOKS LLP
125 A, Ground Floor, Shahpur Jat, Near Asiad Village,
New Delhi–110049, India

First published by Speaking Tiger in hardback 2017

ISBN: 978-93-86050-91-5

10 9 8 7 6 5 4 3 2

Typeset in Adobe Caslon Pro by SÜRYA, New Delhi
Printed at Thomson Press India Ltd.

Contents

People

For Robin the Poet

A bust cast in bronze,
heavy,
and heaved from a millenium of underground sleep,
meditative,
wearing silence like a solitary hermit,
yet you say, 'let's drain the lizard'
when you want to take a piss.

Shit, grime, murder, mediocrity.
How much more must a poet endure
and still keep faith aglow
in the dark lust-paved streets of his brain?

A rush of poems leap from the swaying rice fields
of your childhood and rustle
in the mist-fraught hills of your youth;
speaking first, then whispering the neurosis
of soft breasts breaking a boy into manhood,
of lost identity and collateral butchery,
of greed, revolution, rape, fear, beauty, pain, hope
and of a people living on the margins of a nation's memory.

What words of comfort can you squeeze out
from the nipples of your land?
These armpit towns with their camouflaged agendas
grow ever so covert and treacherous.
Only zealots and martyrs survive here,
the rest may be dispensed with;
or if you are quirky you could be saved
by an entirely unprovoked erection
that temporarily empties you of all conscience
to brave another day
and perhaps return with a poem.

Moonchild

Watch me dance in the moonlight
I'm a child of the moon.
There is clarity at night
and hidden shadows at noon.

Why do you analyse me,
innocent victim of reason?
Your brown eyes can only see,
not perceive this sacred vision.

My life is beyond understanding,
above your enslaving chain.
Untouchable, unbinding,
free from the clever grip of pain.

My lungs are filled with scoffing breath
I ought to leave this place soon.
I who have shed all life and death
laugh with the quiver of the moon.

A Faint Sister of the Moon

(after Dechen Lhamu)

Caught in the dark spaces of time
and unaware
till the first strokes of dawn
bare you to the bone.

Spinning and spinning endlessly
into a gathering storm of incomplete shadows;
except, your eyes have a kind of silence
and you are running.

Do the charred debris of a forbidden fire
still smoulder in some locked chamber of your sleep
to confuse a seed
and taste the bitter fruit of youth?

Your pale arms fade into an embrace
of a terrible loneliness
touched only by the hands of the moon.

Daisy

She's a red balloon
barefoot and airborne
slip sliding in her floating world.
Sometimes she's a firefly
rubbing light from her hand
like a prophet of the times.
But most of all she's a child
showing off a bright new frock
jumping, skipping, spinning,
head thrown back and squeezing
a blue sky from her eyes.

Maggie and I

Cities, you say, bleed you in their hawk-like grip
and this tin-pot town is too casual for expression.
Reposed ever so elegantly with a cigarette, you declare
with a sweep of your hand,
'This place is a piss joint.'

Each year you return from distant lands
gasping for air in brief time packets.
Never caring who you are—unmindful pilgrim—
you could not become sun-clad.

Flicking lights in a dim groan of saxophones,
you tell me cutely, 'I'm lonely without my loneliness,'
but I know you are only drowning in your shadows,
your thin arms splaying into the vortex wind.

And I who have grown like a rock here,
witnessed every grass and cloud that passed;
what kindred hearts we hold
between our strangeness, breathless Maggie,
that we live fugitive lives forever.

Bird of Fire

(after Jimi Hendrix)

Hey bird of fire
return from the ashes.
Your burning hair,
your acid cry
will not cut flesh.
These skins are numb,
these skins are unforgiving.
Leave now without a word,
the desert sun beckons you.
Stop not nor look behind,
the sky knows no fences
and your freedom is absolute.
Go quickly,
there's no confusion.
You, who carries the sirocco under your arms,
keeps the light sparking off your fingers,
will at last be homeward bound.

A Marwari Gentleman Mourns for the Tibet of Yore in the Summer of 1968

They came down across the snow-packed passes,
each mule decorated with bells and tassels.
A leathery faced hardy Tibetan fills the frame
his high boots, braided hair and earrings glinting in the sun.

The Marwari gentleman remembers a time
when whole cars were knocked down and carried over the Himalaya,
like Atlas on nimble feet, and how
Swiss-made watches were packed in gunny sacks
to be bartered for gold and pashmina.

It was a time like no other,
a time festering with ideas,
the intercourse of cultures, the movement of people,
the frenzy for profit.

Years ago his father, and his father before him,
had traded their fates from the sweltering plains of Rajasthan
to strike a fortune in this frozen frontier
wearing only dhotis.

Lhasa gold, they said, would melt in the midday sun,
that's how pure it was.
A family whose turquoise-roofed house
has passed into legend,
where liveried servants in silk brocade and coral beads
waited on them.

Then the red hordes of Mao arrived;
desecration of the sacred was their creed,
revolution a bullet in the head
and paradise spilled daily from the mouth of loudspeakers.

In the dim-lit recesses,
the frescos of Sera and Ganden that for centuries
had conspired for tranquillity
peeled away in one blinding blaze.

From the pages of myth
a country is dragged by its scruff,
its old gentry who picnicked for days
on the banks of the Tsangpo
have since long surrendered their past
into the reality check of a refugee camp.

The Old Monk of Sonada

frail
his shaven head
clean as polished leather

we prostrate

i'm sure I have some clever questions
this time

he smiles…

wrapped in the warmth of his radiance
words quickly dissipate of their meanings

silence sits between us like the firm hand of trust

just before we take leave he says
'be happy!'

suddenly, like a thunder shower,
i know

The Chowkidar

There lives an old man
high up on a far hill.
He is the former chowkidar of the Chakung Dak Bungalow.
Retired many years since
and his profession
passed down three generations to a lad of sixteen,
the new humble chowkidar.

Seated upon a low cane stool
he beckons me to his side.
Then slowly, carefully, unfolding
like a precious heirloom from layers of silk,
he unwraps his enchanting tales
from creation to country
and reveals kings and prophets whose footprints
still bear witness upon rocks
their passage through time.

He desires nothing more
than to pass on the key
to a treasure house of stories
filled with gods, heroes, mountain-spirits,
the long trek of his people,
and a land called *Mayel Lyang*.
His voice is a river of calm,
his eyes misty twin lakes.

In all his countless summers
he has never ventured beyond a day's walk.
I cannot relate to him the world without—
of what use is it to him?
He only knows these encircling mountains,
he only understands the silence within.
Here I am, far from the clamour of existence,
under a blue vaulted sky
dwarfed by this ageless man
walking tall in all his ignorance.

I often return to his tiny world.

Mayel Lyang: The Lepcha refer to Sikkim as Mayel Lyang. It also means paradise.

Jhunkyang: The Last Dream

It's mid-winter and soon time for *Losar*,
time to cast aside our failures and regrets
and propitiate the deities for the New Year.
O take me back to my land of tall mountains and
neighbouring skies,
of serene valleys of rice and trees heavy with oranges.

But alas! You cannot hear me
nor can you read these words of silence
for words have always beguiled me.
Even as I lie here with a hole in my throat,
gazing across the window,
the evening casts giant ugly shadows, distorting facts in this
dying light.

O noble Sakya, holder of the white lotus,
how true are your words on impermanence.
In this final hour I find no greater comfort
than the truth you have spoken.

What a maze the years have been;
from the sunny stills of childhood,
the wild abandonment of youth,
to this dismal hour of separation and pain.
But hear me my gentle people,
though we may be at the ends of the world
and fate unkind to us,
loving you has been my privilege.
And would you believe me if I told you
I've lived these final years lonely for your love?

The first glimmer of neon returns the night to me
and I try to fade into the corners of darkness,
winding spools of memory.
Tonight, the air is dense with the fragrance of home
and I drink once again from the cool springs of my hills,
hear your mirthful laughter rise clear above this commotion.
Farewell, doe-eyed children of the mountains,
remember the promises of our ancestors bound in blood,
and may peace be your pillar of hope.

Look, the dawn is already breaking
and I've carried the night hard on my shoulders.
Now will you allow this old man to unburden quietly?
For he too must sleep the mortal sleep,
though bitter and broken in an alien land.

Chogyal Palden Thondup Namgyal ruled Sikkim between 1965 and 1975. He was deposed and his kingdom annexed under the prime ministership of Indira Gandhi. He spent the remaining part of his life fighting a solitary battle. Unable to speak audibly because of throat cancer, he breathed his last in a New York hospital on 30 January 1982 at 8.00 a.m., succumbing more to sadness than to cancer. However, in recent years, his old subjects have acknowledged his patriotism for his country and today institutes and parks have been renamed in his honour. He was fondly referred to as Jhunkyang by his family, friends and subjects.

Losar: The Tibetan New Year, also celebrated by people of Sikkim and the Palace with great fervour.

Death of a Father (Part I)

For the first time I notice
his eyes are light brown
as they expand with one last light.
All these years
how did they escape me?
Now, every time I gaze into a mirror
I see those eyes look through me.

As his jaws lock tight
my brother tries to unclasp his teeth
to force air into his lungs;
the nurse pounds away at his chest.

Between the wailing, the rain
and a shuffle of doctors…
a final glance;
he leaves through a corridor in the night,
dissolving into intangibles.

And even as that aged body breaks,
snaps every strand of hope,
I register no shock:
except, my prayers flee
faster than my mind can comprehend.

I'm tired, too tired to even
commit to memory
the death of a father.

But these are unsentimental times
and death elicits only practical behaviour.
By the time you are through
taking care of everybody,
your future reads like the back of your hand
and, quite suddenly, without your consent,
you are your father's son.

Death of a Father (Part II)

Because your face
is inside my brain,
those eyes turn slowly over
the landscapes in my dreams,
though your flesh is dust now.

I recall a tough, weathered face
that broke like a child's when *amla*'s coffin arrived
            seven years ago,
that night when marigolds were opening under a bright moon.
Your pain breached a sea of sorrow
and engulfed us all in islands of grief.

The next morning you had
no compass to wake up to,
no centre to anchor upon;
no north, south, east or west
no heaven or earth;
you could find nothing
or
you no longer cared.

And now you are gone too,
leaving us but a coded language—
a row of white shirts and grey pants, a deck of cards,
the steaming aroma of dried fish in black lentil,
a Webley & Scott revolver I sneaked out as a boy,
firing each shot with fearful glee.

This montage of grainy images
is a gift, a medallion
with the dead weight of the past
even as dark shadows split into a pincer movement
to ambush me another day.

Amla: Mother in Bhutia/Tibetan

Of Mothers and Heirlooms

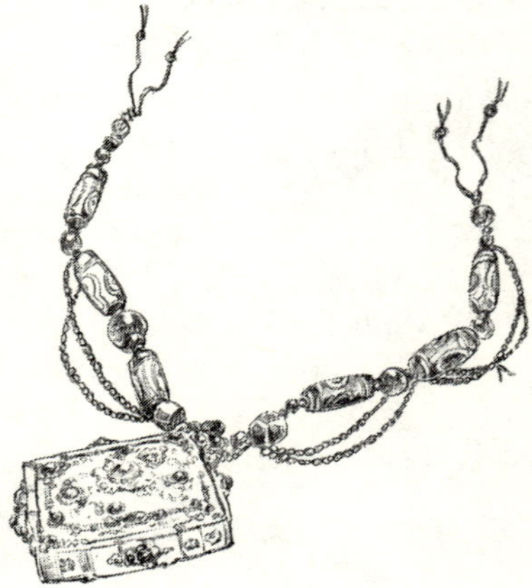

In the right-hand corner of my mother's cupboard is a squat steel safe. Inside you will find red corals freckled with age, one-eyed and three-eyed agates, earrings, heavy bridal *Khao*s inlaid with Tibetan turquoise, pearls unravelled in a silk pouch, a bracelet—the first-ever gift my father bought her, when her wrist was still slim—some rings (some without their stones), an amulet she wore as a child, trinkets, necklaces passed down generations, jewellers' receipts and some horoscope charts rolled up in a corner, unmindful of all the fuss.

I open a large red box, the way she would have on countless occasions, and spread its wares bazaar-like on her bed.

She would pick each piece up, gaze and polish until each gleamed into her past, until the years rose and waved about like a hand and a quiet sun paused briefly on her face. Then suddenly, out of the blue, she would be struck by a mother's anguish: Six grown children in the house and an heirloom to divide them.

Khao: Tibetan/Sikkimese jewellery set worn by women.

The Sikkimese

Amidst talk of El Niño and global warming
a Sikkimese man sticks his tongue out
in a token grimace of fear.

Karma

(young musician, 1989–2010)

The sun in your eyes sparkles—
you are five months old.
How your lanky limbs stretch out of photographs,
getting caught in baggy jeans—
You lean shyly over shoulders.

Youth has cut your face clean
and broken the boyish timbre.
Reclining on the slanting shadows of dusk and desire,
do your hands dream under a pool of melody?

In haste you left to ride the thunder.
In the distance,
your flowing locks plunge among the stars.

O night! shed no tears,
shun, shun the embrace of pain.
Stumbling in the dark,
angels unfurl your wings to harvest the moon tonight.

So here's to you, to your half-lazy smiles
and to laughter in the rain.
Send your mother kisses from a silver sky,
drop me a dozen songs in 12-bar blues.

Funeral at Sohra

(for Mark Gautam who has returned to the wild)

'...because his mind was free,
his humour dark and his hopes ordinary.
His arms opened like the sky above him
without goodbyes;
now he walks tall amongst pines, rivers and wild things.'

When we return from the funeral
some of the women are still crying.
The boys begin drinking in one of the rooms,
careful not to make too much noise.
Daisy's world shuts around her—
there is only so much information she can process.
She floats from room to room
looking for a mysterious key that refuses to open.

It was a beautiful day.
A spotless blue sky that dropped all the way
on to the shimmering plains of Bangladesh.
An almost-smokeless pyre burning on the shoulder of a cliff
overlooking the wettest town in the world.

In the fading light the pyre-tenders stoke the fire—
their sweaty skins reflect the rouge of the dying embers.
As the crowd slowly thins away
the pyre-tenders and hangers-on conclude the day
with free-flowing *kakiyad* and loud, mundane talk.
In the din and the dust no one notices a shining star collapse
into a corner of the sky.

Tonight there is that much less light.

Depature

(a sister's lament)

In *Nia*'s dream you stood outside her house,
requesting permission to enter.
Your tall frame, your impeccable words
falling softly like leaves in autumn.
Someday my daughters will ask about you,
and I will struggle to tell them
of your departure.

My dreams have since blacked out.
The pathways of branching nerves
have severed at the roots.
I should have never identified your body—
a jigsaw of limbs and a torso,
a single shoe, your buck teeth without a face
and a cigarette lighter inside one of your pockets,
inscribed,
'near or far, you're always in my heart,
love, Carrie.'
The only reason I did not collapse was because
Vik kept telling me,
'That's not our brother, it's just a lump of meat.'

In the wake of your departure you have left
a mother battered by insomnia,
clinging to the sheets you slept on,
and a father unhealed, grasping at shadows,
hoping to make amends.

I reject your relentless absence.

Those long summer days
camped at the riverside, you cut such a dashing figure,
cool in your sunglasses and casting the fly line so skillfully—
I was so proud.

Please come back,
and rid me of this stench of the morgue
that refuses to go away.

Nia: Aunt in the Khasi language.

Regret

(reply to a sister's lament)

No one waters the roses around the porch any more.
The rooms are cold, the wooden floors unpolished,
our mother is but a fading shadow
dragged around the house by an involuntary breath.
My leap to freedom, my flight from pain
has left you insomniac,
muting the syllables in your throat,
unable to rationalize the razor's bite
even as the bulk of an enormous night festers.

I thought no one would understand
and your heart's loneliness is unforgiving.
Cheated by light, my reality refracted between air, water and earth,
distortion and delusion seeped slowly into my being.
Death's seduction came easy.

But the truth is we do not die,
Here, too, we mark the beginning of a cyclical journey.
I still walk lonely on the other side,
wearing regret like a red scarf.

How does one write apologies to so many broken souls?
Can I tell you how splendid a spring morning is,
or how the tug of mahseer on a line still gets me;
the camaraderie of men which lifts high over a meandering river?

Above all, you, my most dearest,
do not validate hopelessness,
never let this tremble of life escape you,
however fragile and unappreciated it may yet appear.

A Forlorn Monsoon Afternoon

(for Steve Namchu, former lead guitarist, Route 66)

Mist everywhere,
pervasive,
dissolves the shapes of my room.
A naked incandescent bulb hangs over a grey afternoon.

Down in the valley the Teesta swells and snarls full-bellied
like a mythical beast
frothing brown spray from its many mouths.

A jeepload of people hurtle down a ravine.
Tyres squeal; suddenly, the soft earth buckles underneath and
snuffs out nine lives.
Some onlookers narrate the terrible scene to more onlookers;
their pants rolled up to their ankles, their necks craned
under umbrellas,
trace the fatal fall and resign themselves to fate's implacable will.

This bleak day of incessant rain
soaks my mind colourless
and my thoughts turn slowly to Steve,
up on a hillside under a freshly dug grave
alone and cold
with no warm arms around him.

Monk on a Hill

A brand-new road burrows its way up this trail;
what use is it to an old monk on a hill?
Except, our lands and rivers will be up for sale
and my people drunk on easy money for a summer.
The low hum of engines from the valley below,
the rat-a-tat of machines on rocks
invade my wooden hut at the forest's edge.

Not a single cloud gathers over a crested horizon,
time measures itself with the fullness and the fall of fruit.
Green stalks of rice bend in the early autumn breeze,
the scent of large cardamom floats in upon woodsmoke.
Even in this serene, still solitude,
this mind can still be all a-chatter.

As a child I was a little devil, I'm told,
always jumping, climbing, breaking bones,
until my suffering parents surrendered me to a monastery.
Four score and one this November,
that restless child still remains—
impatient, foolish, and a pair of quick feet for distant shores,
though it's been long since I last crossed the Teesta.

The dusk soon blots out the colours of the land,
smudging the outline of the hills with night's ink.
The shrill drone of cicadas relay from bush to tree;
a flutter of wild wings settle down to roost,
a flicker of lamps dot the darkening lands
closing another day upon this sacred soil of our forebears.

I have no regrets,
tomorrow is just another day.
Snow on the mountains, a rustle of leaves in the woods,
a pot of tea on the boil and verses from the Heart Sutra.
What more can a silly old man want?
Until the rhododendrons bloom again,
you will find me, none the wiser, plodding that old path
which disappears into the far bamboo grove.

Vincent

(at the Musée d'Orsay)

Under the incandescent orb of a museum light
I am pinned by your eyes
against a cobalt sky.
Your mind is a vortex
your hair a hurricane.
The placid lake of your ancient heart
waits endlessly across the far mountains
and I have come to your raging wheat fields
under a burst of black crows,
my breath sinking in the swirl.

I am here
in the expanse of your frame
amidst a blue scream and a pause,
the energy of yellow and the weight of ochre
all yielding to an urgency—burning and consuming forever
without release.

In the Words of Socheat

(a tribute to the countless victims of Khmer Rouge)

They kill my father,
they kill my mother in front of house.
My sister very beautiful, soldier take her
she cry and she fall on ground,
but soldier drag her to army truck.
I don't know where they take.
She said, '*Aun Proh*, you take care of yourself now.'
That time I only nine year old, I don't know how take care.
Life very hard for me,
many time I eat what others throw,
just like pig.
No home, no family, no food.
I now forty seven years
but I remember that day like yesterday.
I see big man of Khmer Rouge on TV,
many little grandchildren with him,
he old now and many TV reporters outside his house.
He not talk to anyone but tell his grandchildren many stories,
they laugh, hold his hand and run around.
But he not tell my story,
the story of orphan dog.
Other day police arrest him and take to Phnom Penh
to face international court.
But he weak, he no longer strong,
even no can walk properly.
They say, this is wheel of Karma
and no one can escape.
Before he very powerful, killing people like flies,

he not care how many he kill,
just kill only.
Now they take him,
all his family cry, little children block his way and say,
'Grandpa, don't go, stay with us, we love you.'

I also cry a little.

Aun Proh: Term of endearment for a younger brother in Khmer.

The D. L. Effect

Drawing from deep wells of joy
he breaks into loud, hearty laughter.
It hangs over us like sunshine
till our faces glow a ridiculous pink
and we are left wondering
why an entire crowd inside
an indoor stadium is grinning silly.
It's like we are all on something, man.

Swans soaring over the Potala
on an autumn night
will remain a youthful memory for now;
and the slow genocide of his people
a blunt reminder of power that corrupts absolutely.
But right here, there's no stopping this heaving humanity
from 'not-getting-enough'
till the doors explode.

Okay, not all prophets walk on water,
or have such comic gift,
but he sure has a way of unshackling your mind
and inducing zero gravity
so you soar beyond the arc of the sun
like a breath on a child's wish—dipping and diving into the blue.
He does so by means of no extraordinary feat,
only through a simple appreciation
of every moment
and every life.

Places

Ladakh

Where the dashing jawline of the Karakoram
crushes onto the broad shoulders of the Himalaya,
this land, my namesake,
lifting above the clouds.

In this desolate country
who hewed these stones to arch?
The unknown artists of Alchi
painting the eyes of *Maitreya*
steal glimpses through the lens of time.
The sheer determination of the ramparts of Hemis
            betray a quiet awe;
the plain of Changthang is the wind in my hair.

Here, before a naked sky and earth,
everything is broken down to basics,
need is reduced to the simple arithmetic
of survival,
joy enhanced by the straightforward rejection
of want.

This land of saints and salt traders
clings to my mornings
like an umbilical cord
bequeathed by a lost ancestor.

Maitreya: The future Buddha

Manipur

(for Robin S. Ngangom)

'Ten hacked to death,
six shot dead with their hands tied to their back!'
A grey man informs us with a formal face
over breakfast.
A thousand miles away, what do we know?
We quietly finish our bread and eggs
and flip channels.

Slowly, the images take shape,
I pick out two faces from my campus days
whom I have not remembered in years.
One not particularly bright,
the other only played football.
Such unlikely candidates, I should imagine,
for the Kalashnikov brigade
have now had their fates writ
in some waterlogged, tropical terrain,
erased in one rapid, unguarded moment.

Manipur, I'll never pretend to understand you.
Your festering wounds, your bald cry
bring only a sense of failure to us.
I seek the words of my friend,
a shy child of your valley and hills,
who weaves me into his voice
and takes me on a journey
through the labyrinths of a hard country
to arrive each time at bitter truths
until your pain is stitched bright over my heart.

Journey to Bodh Gaya

An overnight train chugs
into the heart of darkness.
Insomnia—
the engine hisses and wails
at every nondescript station
for the umpteenth time
until we arrive at a morning that
refuses to lift.

We change transport
and drive through the heartland of India.
Turbaned trucks hurtle in and out of the morning fog,
shawled men atop cargoes
move forever on the highway.

'This is open country,' my wife observes,
bracing herself to connect the unfolding images.
'Here I see people bathe in the open,
cook in the open, defecate in the open, and quite literally
live their lives in the open.'
Outside my car window the land
juxtaposes a cruel dichotomy—
fertile fields of plenty and the hopelessness of poverty.

'Bodh Gaya 0 km,' the milestone reads,
revealing a different country, a different sun.
More foreigners than locals mill about;
a crush of pilgrims, touts, hawkers, guides,
fervent converts singular in their devotion
behind a monk robed in ochre and saffron.

A banner catches my eye:
'Be Vegetarian for Happy, Healthy and Humane World—
Tibetans for a Vegetarian Society.'
A group of Tibetans scratch their heads before the banner
and smile like children caught doing something naughty.

The moon rises over the Great Temple
and, under the Bodhi Tree,
the night is absorbed by a thousand lamps.
Amidst muffled footsteps and falling leaves,
for a fleeting moment,
great peace.

At this very spot,
two-and-a-half millennia ago,
rose a man to change the path of mankind.

Kalimpong Revisited

Straddled upon a ridge,
this quaint town
winds her narrow streets into my adolescence,
heaving long, ponderous schooldays,
and fills my nostrils with memories
that leapfrog into the present.

I meet faces that have shed their names
and shops that have slept through the decades;
their owners still greet me
with a certain tone and gesture
unchanged in all these years.

This far-flung post of the Raj,
shaped inside secret rooms of geo-politics
on the whim of an Empire
opened her thighs from the border of a century
to traders, missionaries, spies, scholars,
all looking for their private little haven.

Once a gateway to Central Asia,
now reduced to a second-class destination
for low-budget tourists who come claiming
their own space, loud with cameras,
but can never quite capture her elegant past
alive only in the stories of her fading custodians.

Main Road, Mela Ground, Eleventh Mile
mark their own stones again
leading me somewhere in my head,
to a place that time forgot—
a beaten path arched by bougainvilleas.
I enter a world fraught with dreams.

Kohima

In the market square
a swirl of emblazoned *mekhlas*
hug the hips of laughing virgins,
interrupted neither by sky
nor by the ancient fires
burning in deep jungle camps.

On a crisp December afternoon
nobody forewarns an oblivious passerby—
the heavy rustle of khaki and metal
steals under a sharp night
bristling with brutality.

I choose only to hear the melodious guitar
stroke its fingers over a child's sleep-filled eyes.
Tonight I shut myself out from the gunfire
and collapse in your embrace so tight,

your each breath is still damp
on the rim of my memory.
And all through the night I want to forget
who is right and who survives.

For tomorrow yet another from the lost generation
will follow a blood trail to the top of the hill
to bear the Cross for a few wise men.

Shillong, 1992

There is a moon tonight
over the skies of Shillong.
From my drive to the peak,
I can see the city dipped in a fluorescent glow,
simmering sensuality and neon sophistication.

Yet I feel utterly deceived
for my friend walks the streets of hatred everyday,
terror thrashing in his guts,
and my poet-brothers write sad verses
of the lost innocence of these hills,
where carefully nurtured fear runs amok and,
on a beautiful Sunday morning,
a skull breaks open on soft dew-laden grass.

Here, all around me, I bear grim witness to the cancer
that stalks your narrow lanes
and sucks hollow the freshness out of life.
I weep as one hill man to another.

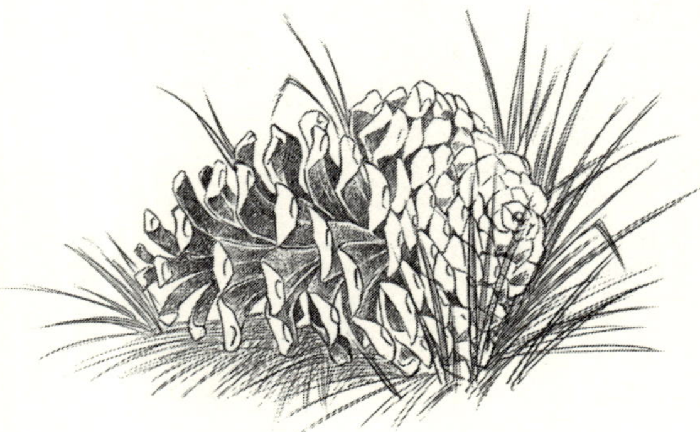

Farewell, Shillong, I came because you beckoned
but I must leave now,
for the songs on your lips have died
and you live clinging to the ghost of yesterday.

Nongkhnum

After a furious downpour at five
we begin our trek
with only the bare essentials—
beer, cigarettes and roast meat—
to commemorate a day
of no significant occasion.

Under a freshly washed April sky
flanked by a waterfall plunging to my right,
duelling in-laws to my left
and a Kodak chrome day bunking beyond the horizon.

Daisy—grandmother, single, buoyant,
can never offer solitude the same reverence as shopping,
braves the surreptitious path in her heels.
Mark, eBay survivor and, intermittently,
Oracle of Interesting but Unproductive Information,
would rather live at the wedge of a confluence,
dreaming of the big one that got away,
and Priya,
my wife of less than a year
unaware of a pea-sized life
rapidly colonizing her insides,
have all claimed me for this journey.

Bucolic landscape, fresh grass,
and yonder a river encircling a hill
to assert the dubious title of
'The second largest river island in Asia'.
Sand in my pants,
I get up to chill the beer in the river.

Nongkhnum is in Meghalaya. Although not verified, it is considered to be the second largest river island in Asia.

Candolim, Goa, a Reflection (January 2013)

They drowned,
swallowed by the sun
the sea
and twenty heads staring clueless.
'She is gone too mate, you can't do nothing now,' said a
        beefy Aussie
as he unclasped his mouth after a failed resuscitation.
Like two whales beached on hot sand
they lay aside each other,
still frothing like strange sea creatures.

From the deep cow belt of India, they had sought a vacation
on this slice of paradise on azure seas.
The wife, shy, afraid, waving anxiously from the shore.
The husband, big and burly, braving the waves in his fading
        underwear,
which never elicits raised eyebrows amongst us Indians.

In less than ten minutes after we passed them
a world turned topsy-turvy.
Seduced by the sea,
the wife timidly joins her husband.
The cool hands of the sea stroke gently at first
till they are lulled away and abandon caution;
the first big wave knocks them over,
then a second and a third;
the pounding seems unending and panic is a deadly killer.
Water, water, water all around.

Her kurta pulled up for CPR reveals stretch marks.
Unbeknown to their children
running across the fallow fields or the crowded streets
of north India,
two rainbows lie broken on this beach
while the police loudspeaker
makes half-hearted attempts to break the crowd,
then drives away in a wail of sirens.

I do not know how I should feel.
Do I feel sad, lucky that it wasn't us
or angry at the lifeguards
who did not know what they were doing?
Or do I pause at this breath so fleeting?

I watch for long…
the waves casting and returning in the distance,
the moon sailing high above the palm trees
and beyond the tourist shacks,
the silence of the night suspended between water and light.

Where are my words that map the contours of loss?
The night caves in, drowning a pitiful day,
leaving neither shape nor sound.

Africa

Your blue waters are soothing
and your mountains rise up to a sky moist with hope.
The rearview mirror of our Volkswagen
hangs waves of grassland quickly receding
from a thin memory of glass till, past the bush country,
I arrive only to browse at my own questions.

Will my brother pinning new stars
over the shacks and kraals
look to the future,
or unlock the gates in his head,
succumbing darkly to fear,
closing rank and file,
eyes locked into fists?

Yes, I have come parting the oceans
to hear your drums
and trace the footprints of Adam
walking on the horizon of time
from the heartlands of Africa.

Seasons

Monsoon

Two clouds walk with moist feet
over the shoulders of the opposite hill,
picking sunshine from the undergrowth.

The rains keep us indoors, mostly,
tossing the bones of forgotten promises
that lie at the doorway,
like ancient servants who summon themselves
between damp hours with tea and biscuits.

Autumn

Khangchendzonga sprawls along the horizon
cool in a fresh jacket of snow.
Throat covered in a scarf of clouds,
and whispering among the pines some hints of winter.

Rivers sieve away their bulging bellies
flowing once again
limpid and trim at the waist.

Buoyant upon drumbeats
a chorus of eager feet try to match
the rhythm, voice and soul of *Teohar*

Opening the second cherry blossom
I slide along the slopes of her moods
and find myself lying wide-eyed
under a high noon of a thousand marigolds.

Teohar: Nepali festival

Winter

Vehicles returning from border towns
lift snow on their tarpaulin roofs
and take over M. G. Marg in a white parade.
The mercury dips to just above zero
and can you beat it,
the capital is without electricity
for the third day in a row!

I reach home sharpening my frustration
and quickly disappear under layers of blankets.
We eat dinner in bed.

As a pall of gloom covers the ground,
the northern hemisphere slants farther from the sun.

Sleep arrives finally with a passport in its pocket.
I lean over palm fronds and ocean surf
and sink my face upon brown breasts.

Haiku

full moon
crowns a fig tree
Siddhartha's final awakening

~

thunderstorm sky
my father sits
a solid mountain

~

all morning
clouds climb up the valley
my tea-kettle whistles

~

forest fire
through the night
quiet flows the niranjan

~

winter's day
long shadows of a pale sun
a robin's simple song

~

green bamboos
sway in the summer breeze
scent of mangoes

~

darkening sky
rumble of distant thunder
temple gong

~

stars dim
a friend's passing heaps memories
burden of the living

Postscript

Desire

Desire is a dog
breathing
roaming the streets all day long.

The moon-stroked curves of your body
carved by a keen blue night.
Breasts dip a secret hand
thighs open among vines
the scent of a heady fruit.

And seasons change without respite.

I was once a young man
with arrows in my tongue
who could pin your wings down
and pour all the love and loathing
I could gather.

Finetime

heard the sound of a rainbow
tingle inside my ears
felt the coat of its colours
brush under my fingertips
tasted the spectrum of light
dissolve upon my tongue
blinded by ten thousand rainbows
arched in the sky

you can say
i'm high on you

Retrospect

Death is simpler than dying.
The coffin rolls in and rolls out
and so with droves of people
who hand over money* like morbid gifts.

We hardly have a sense of loss
till all the chairs, cups and spoons are returned
and the echo of the last footfall softens,
descending one grey morning in brief parachutes.

A thick thud of epiphany wakes us like a hand
fixing our breath in a frame.
Slowly turning upon your absence
that stretches ahead like an empty highway.

How peculiar an outcome
that this death should reject all reciprocity
between us save a retrospect
at every point of reference.

---

*Money is offered by mourners as part of condolences in Sikkimese society.

Sub merger

(*...so a spirit without root is an injustice.*
It rejects the beauty that is offered it.)

Pablo Neruda (Exile)

I toddled a winding path yesterday
through a forest of voices,
borrowed landscapes, strange hats and funny lingo.
(did I choose? was there a choice?)
Bubble feet rising to the crest
and dreaming another man's dream,
we have become such agreeable exiles in our own land.
In this surge of time,
the ocean tides climb the mountains.
Are we to be submerged in the sea forever, brother?
What hands played the cosmic dice
to chance this harsh sarcasm
that tonight I stand amidst the waters,
a shell in hand,
trying to trap a lost wind of the hills
from uncertain leagues under the sea?

A Night in a Café

Cigarettes pressed to your face
you try to singe the nerves of pain.
For a moment it is almost analgesic:
exhaling memories through jets of smoke.

At a corner table I finish my last sip of brandy
and the waiter shuffles polite hints.
Will you stop by this stranger
and bury your fears in his arms?

The empty street that stretches ahead
into a soft filter of sodium vapour and mist
awaits, keen as a premonition,
and shuts its eyes.

Two days later I hear you are recovering
from a night of exit wounds.

A Desultory Day in a Life

His head still in a fog after a night's binge,
he begins his day from the crossroads of his bed.
He thinks he should just stick to beer.

        a car below goes into spasm on a bright April morning

Books, tapes, empty bottles lie strewn everywhere.
Through a slight window
a dog stretches full
flexing the afternoon a little.

        the phone rings—
        the vacant hour expands in sonorous ripples

Hey, a ghost from the past is calling
from across a sandy shore in the Mediterranean.
She's all accent and information
and is quick with an invitation.

        beyond the doors in his head
        the scent of a citrus country is drifting

He walks down two hundred feet of newly built steps
of idiotic shapes and measurements,
first cussing then reconciling to the incorrigible.
But before he relents he goes pot shooting all the lamps along
        the path.

        a dark delight escapes his grin

Tonight he calls upon a girl, a classmate from high school,
whose endless legs had given him his first serial bout of erections.
She's now an officer, single and leggier.
They are alone in the room
and she's very polite.

the night heaves from her hips and buttocks

Running his gaze across the walls, floorboards,
chairs, coffee table, picture frames
he arrives upon her round firm breasts
rising and falling rhythmically.

his hands feel a sudden request
his breath is a rapid leopard

Unbuttoning his shirt with a poker face
he says, 'Do you know how hot it is right now?'

Novice

(to a silence more meaningful than any word
to a stillness more powerful than any activity)

—The Message of the Tibetans

i'm not sad
nor am I happy,
if you ask me,
i'm just okay

ideas and noise
don't crowd anymore,
only eating, sleeping,
walking, talking

and waiting above all
for my silence
to speak and perhaps
start things anew

but for now
i'm occupied fulltime
trying to teach myself
to do nothing

The Late Cherry

For most of the year she recedes into the
backdrop
of grey concrete, glass and tin
drowned as she is by the din
of traffic at Zero Point pressed to a
full stop.

Her sleep is deep and breaks a quarter annum
later
than her siblings but in a scream,
blood-red hair and peeling a dream
from her eyelids; the falling skins of a hard
winter.

How many times have you awoken from such a
slumber
to survey at the crossroads
slow mules that file with pack loads
give way to motor gods and write off an era
forever.

Or do your roots sipping from a vast pool of
memory
foretell after a light shower in early spring
of fading dynasties and images they fling
at a people who have chosen to forget their
history.

Growing Up and a Hailstorm

In this fierce beating of hailstones
I feel a light transport
to where I'm neatly arranged
in a pair of bleached canvas shoes
racing down tall corridors of my school.
Not yet ten
and already asking too many questions.
There among excited voices that surround
the ground is a swelling of white bouncing pellets.
As I slide a fistful of ice
down her back
I become painfully conscious
for the first time of touch.
My senses stretch
from skin to her lavender breath.
Imagine what ignorance I risk
as I follow through her request
scrupulously
to the last desk.
She holding my hand so tight
I dissolve quickly into
a vocabulary of silence.

Ranbandhu

I see you are travelling light, my friend
no baggage in your hand.
You've got a one-way ticket out of here.
Your wings leave no trace over the northern skies
save for a clarity in your sapphire eyes.

As you soar you begin to shed all duality,
radiant is your golden hair.
Then, bending low, you softly speak,
'What we receive is equal to what we give up.'
I lick the sun from your morning cup.

Ranbandhu: A stranger turned spiritual friend with whom you share a karmic connection that goes back many lifetimes.

Blue Notes

Two bodies stretch into the night
angled across a bed of languor
to exclude
the warmth of each others' arms.
Jaded memories gather around a defunct fire
unable to shake the words
pressed under the heels of a dead night.

The morning is a long time coming
to resolve this peculiar matter of sleeping postures
in an ageing partnership.

Scar

As I write to you
I let this page re-examine a scar,
a slender and bleached outgrowth
that sticks onto your narrow wrist.

You once sought this very scar
as the gateway to end all pain.
It now encloses two lives
within the walls of a frozen wound.

What I Dread

What I dread most about you
is that you will understand me
for having pursued women with large breasts
and kissing their legs in quaint rooms
that follow me beyond the traffic of time
with their odour-heavy addresses.
Now you, unfastening with patient and clean hands
your scarless affection;
of that I am afraid.

If you must love me,
keep for me a shadow knitted upon your brow
and walk me to the tiger in your heart
that licks its paws and locks me in its eyes
only because it feels alive
to live a little dangerously
like an unyielding riddle upon your palm.

A Himalayan Ballad

Across the wind-filled pass of Nathu
In the valley of the orange country
Lives the mother of my child-to-be.
Do not grieve, my love.
At Shigatse I've bought you a turquoise ring.
In the holy temple of Lhasa
I'll offer butter lamps and silk scarves.
White cranes flying south to the plains of Phakpay-yul,
Bear the tidings of this rootless trader.
Tell her I'll come speeding on my Yarcund mare
If at year-end business should prove fair.

O father of my child, come soon!
Today your son uttered your name.
You left on the eve of the last peach blossom
And now their fallen hues collect about our bamboo gate.
The tinkle of caravans from the north
Takes me running as far as the crossroads.
How I wish it were you.
Everybody clicks their tongue when they see me.
I cannot think of work, I think only of you.
By next spring your son will be walking
And asking for you. What will I say?
Maybe when you return you can take me along, too.
But alas, I do not have warm shoes to follow you.

World Cup

Ten to fifteen kids, all drinking, smoking, slapping
and swearing over a World Cup semi-final match.
I tell my son I'm trying to sleep.
His eyes disregard,
and then reject everything about me.
Some twenty-five years ago
those same eyes would search my face,
and from those freckled cheeks
each vowel would rise up to the sky like a balloon.

My fever returns, tempers flare;
all I remember is him pointing his finger at his crotch.
Then a moment sits forever on the edges of a world beyond
and this night forfeits all its mornings.
A sudden pool of dark deep blood
expands like a map of a conquering general
and exerts its borders across the floor.
Flashes of screams follow, people scurry away like mice.
In the centre of the room
a *khukuri* lies buried deep inside soft flesh.

Elsewhere, a heaving humanity rides along on a wave of cheer.
Elsewhere, new stars are flickering across the continents.

---

khukuri: A curved knife broadening towards the point, used by Gurkhas, soldiers and menfolk of Nepali origin.

If

If my tears had no roots,
they could exit without a plaintiff's claim.
If expectation remained a mere figment of my imagination,
or yours,
I could lie here on this couch for eternity
and not lift a finger.
If giving was all I knew
and taking was just a walk in the woods,
holding hands.
If we could make love with tenderness
and not think of the morning which will send us
asunder onto a forked path.
If grief was a clown's painted face
and our brains so wired they could
actually connect sans agendas.
If fate was a freight train that knocked me down,
every time
and still, I wouldn't rage against broken signals.
I could kiss your feet like Jesus
and gladly surrender my flesh to the cross
rather than navigate through the dark tunnels of your mind
that breathes no syllables of light,
empty of human touch
and hacking at every bone of the universe.

Lhamu's Scar

For years Amla would agonize over a scar on my sister's forehead. Duplicating my aerial feat, Lhamu trips in mid air, falling like a drunk on the edge of a bed. Blood splatters and her cries summons a mother in her tigress avatar.

I, too, have scars but they never seem to bother my mother. Cuts and nicks on my knees and elbows, some the size of coins, and others embedded like fossils under thighs and forearms. But the one I flaunt like a tattoo runs diagonal over my eyebrow. For a boy of eight it came with unexpected benefits; it elicited a certain reverence and lent itself to a dark, brooding image. I was quite unsure if it was good or bad. 'Cool' hadn't quite entered this kid's lexicon yet.

'A girl's face is her fortune.' Amla did not utter these words, but she didn't have to. She died too young to live out her anxieties. Would Lhamu's suitors, pursuing their separate affections, be acutely aware of her scar? Would catty match-making aunts visiting a prospective bride slip in snide remarks between cups of tea? Or would Lhamu charm them all, cleverly hiding her silver stitch?

I remember: On many such days Amla would gaze far beyond her dressing mirror, combing my sister's hair, running her fingers absently over the protrusion as if each stroke would somehow erase the bristles of this shining, sleeping, breathing pain.

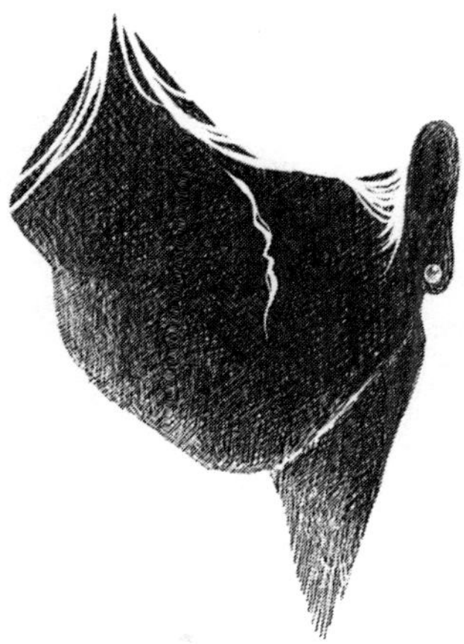

A Constant Lover

Two black shoes descend from a window frame, a blue school tunic, a pair of pink ribbons and a freckled face. The teenager is already made awkward by her swelling breasts. I have seen her grow, seen her body break shyly into womanhood. The years waste away but I'm there every morning at my window.

She appears every once in a while, her blue school tunic long outgrown. Her rotund buttocks, her endless thighs lost deep inside secret gardens, her cascading locks gather monsoon clouds overhead. In no time a baby is groping at her breasts.

Sometimes we exchange glances on M. G. Marg. She practices a faux recollection out of politeness, her mouth curving into a smile, a Sikkimese grace; but on such nights I recline on a sickle moon with a leg dangling gently over a million stars.

At Pema's wedding she unloads like a sack, spilling years of accumulated calories across the sofa. But the remnants of that old beauty still rekindle the embers of lust. Her two teenage kids, impervious to their surroundings or me, add nothing to that memory. They look bored and vacant throughout.

You don't know how many times I have replayed in my head a single life-altering moment; the things I would say and how she would peer into my soul and gently slip her hand into mine. Nothing happens, except time peters away like sand through my fingers.

Who will remember my ardour and chronicle my penance, will anyone write an epitaph on my constant love? I have since been deceased for a quarter of a century. I'm that aching ghost, floating under the dark side of the moon, moving among shadows, still haunted by those first visuals—two black shoes, a blue school tunic, a pair of pink ribbons and that freckled face.

Epilogue

Once I kept your name under my tongue
and whistled it like a song.
Now I've found the ease of smiles,
the safety in formality,
die-cast in exact phrases.
I've learnt to spit out the residue of lilies
every morning mechanically with toothpaste.
I've avoided the fire,
become blind to your provocative eyes.
I've walked the length of my days,
stood at a corner of the world,
and watched distance swallow up the miles,
yet felt neither separation nor union,
nor pain, nor joy
only this boundless space,
this resounding emptiness
with pieces of sky stuck over my eyes.
No, I'll not belong,
there is nothing more to give
I've exchanged everything I ever possessed for
nothing.

Special Thanks

When I began writing verse in my late teens, I had a vague feeling, if not an outright realization, that I would not see a collection published before my fortieth birthday. I made my estimate simply on the basis of my poor prolificacy; one which, I suppose, is anathema to would-be career writers. This volume has come a decade after my fortieth birthday. And it would perhaps have never materialized had it not been for the constant reminders and encouragement by friends and well-wishers. Hence my thanks are due to all these wonderful people.

Anurag Basnet, for recognizing my poetry as an editor. Robin Ngangom, who is a mentor and a long-time friend. Priya, my wife, whom I would not have met had she not been dragged to a poetry reading by a friend. My two daughters whose unconditional love inspires me, and my many siblings whose loyalty binds us whole. The Converse Collectif which gives me succour and reason. Raman Shrestha of Rachna Books for his gentle reminders. Tashi Chopel, a fellow poet whose collection I keenly look forward to. Vishal Kesari for his steadfastness. The late Emu Foning, one of the founders of Converse in 1998, for her guidance. And, above all, Pankaj Thapa, who has not only sketched all the amazing illustrations in this book, but also connected me to the group of Shillong Poets and the larger writing fraternity—that has made all the difference.